Thrive

# A to B Guide to

# Delegation

Brian Guest

Thrive

Thrive Careers Ltd.

www.thrive-careers.com

# ABOUT THRIVE

Thrive Careers specializes in providing leading career development information, mentoring and coaching products and services to professionals and corporate clients around the world.

Created to support managers and executives with their career challenges and development objectives, Thrive is at its core a promoter of self-development and effective leadership.

This guidebook series, along with Thrive's other product ranges, are designed to suit the objectives and busy schedules of modern day professionals by providing cost-effective expertise, interactivity and flexibility to clients. For more information on our other guidebooks, self-assessment tools, coaching and mentoring products visit our website:

www.thrive-careers.com

Thrive Careers Ltd. is based in London, United Kingdom.

# THRIVE A TO B GUIDEBOOKS

This series is written for managers and executives who wish to develop their core skills and those of their teams.

Each guidebook draws on the practical experience of a top executive coach and senior business leader. This breadth of experience helps you see the bigger picture and provides state-of-the-art thinking and tools for achieving positive and sustainable change.

In this series Thrive aims to support and challenge you in your learning and development with a blend of coaching and mentoring approaches. Not only does this grant you access to top quality resources derived from in-depth experience, but also frames them in a way that you can relate to your own circumstances and challenges.

Executive coaching is one of the most powerful and effective ways for leaders and managers to develop their skills and performance. But working one-to-one with a top coach is not always feasible.

The A to B guides give you access to several of the advantages of coaching in a cost-effective and just-in-time approach. You will be constantly challenged to assess your own situation – where you want to get to and how best to get there. It's all about achieving results effectively, efficiently, economically and sustainably. To do this you will be using tools that top professional coaches use with their clients to help you coach yourself and others. You will also be challenged to find the changes that are going to give you the biggest improvement and given advice on how to tackle diverse situations you may encounter.

The series is designed to be easy to work through and to store most of your key notes and plans so that they become working documents. This aspect, coupled with the common structure and layout, make them easy to refer back to and to sustain your learning and progress.

# CONTENTS

# GETTING THE MOST OUT OF THIS RESOURCE

- Consider your overall work context and write down your major challenges. This will help to give context and priorities to the development of your delegation.

_____

_____

_____

_____

_____

_____

- Review the overall structure first.

- Go through the guidebook in sequence, completing the exercises and self-assessments as set out.

- Get feedback from others as suggested.

- Mark areas you wish to return to think about or understand more fully.

- Highlight areas you believe could be key to your own progress and that resonate strongly with you.

- Follow the guide to producing your own developmental goals using the Challenge-Priority Brainstorming Chart and Thrive Action Plan located in the appendix of this guidebook. Be positive and get going!

- Create a mentor or thinking partner relationship at work to challenge and support you on your journey: someone who you believe has and deserves a good reputation in the area of your developmental need.

- Consider creating a small focus group to meet periodically and share thoughts on particular challenges and dilemmas any of you are facing in this area of development.

- Incorporate a reread of the guide into your action plan.

# THE A TO B METHODOLOGY

The A to B methodology is based upon the premise that we have the ability to change and develop in the ways that we really want to.

There are four key questions:

- Where am I? This is "**A**." This sometimes has an element of being "stuck" about it – think of it as a red stoplight impeding you from continuing your journey.

- Where do I need to get to? This is "**B**." Imagine it as the blue sky you see when you reach the top of a mountain that makes you realize just how much you've achieved throughout your journey.

- What barriers are in my way and how can I overcome them?

- What else do I need "**TO**" get there? Think of this as the green traffic light that has come on to let you progress with your journey.

Where you are is where you are. **A** is **A**. It helps to accept this gracefully. Some things have gone well and perhaps some things could have gone better. We can calmly learn from the past, but we cannot let it keep absorbing us, especially if the emotions it evokes are negative for us. Some unwanted or disliked things might seem present in **A**, they may seem to be out of our control. How we react to them inside ourselves, however, is ultimately under our control.

Imagine holding where you are, represented by a big letter **A**, in the open relaxed palm of your left hand (or right hand if you are left-handed), and where you are going, represented by a big letter **B**, in your other palm, which is raised up a foot higher than the other palm. You need to let go of any strong emotions about **A** and feel excited and positive about improving to **B**.

You have particular strengths and development needs. These can depend on circumstances, both inside yourself – for example, your mood, stress or energy levels – or in your external environment – for example, the pressures in your particular business.

Sometimes we can accurately understand our actual position. Sometimes we need input or feedback from others to see our position more clearly. We may think we are clear and communicative delegators but those we delegate to will be aware of our shortcomings in this area.

We learn best by leveraging our strengths – our learning preferences and building on our positive experiences and talents. Very often we see the glass as half-empty instead of half-full. A positive attitude is important in making progress.

Next you need to know where you want to get to. This needs to be a better place; better in terms of what you value. It might not be perfect, but it is better and will meet most of your priority needs.

Finally, you need a clear plan for what you need to do to get to that better place. You need to identify the challenges and support or resources you need to grow and develop into the new position.

# 1. WHAT IS DELEGATION?

## 1.1    Derivation

The word delegation comes from the Latin word "delegare" that means
to send-off or assign a task to someone. The origin of the word may have
come from Roman landowners assigning errands to laborers and send-
ing them away to complete them, but the modern-day meaning is deeper.
In the current world of business a manager needs a broader and deeper
range of skills to make the most of delegation. We shall see this more
clearly as the guidebook progresses.

## 1.2    Management definition

With the above definition in mind, delegation is therefore the practice of
entrusting someone with a particular task and giving them the responsibility and authority required to accomplish such a task.

A delegator generally has the overall accountability for accomplishing
a task, but doesn't execute it. This releases the delegator to co-ordinate
and work on other tasks, as well as to manage the broader objectives
under their responsibility. Ideally, delegation is made through agreement
between the parties that feeds off a constructive relationship of trust,
respect and openness. Delegation is therefore also about reaching agreement and the positive exchange of information.

When delegating an assignment there should be a mutual agreement
between the parties involved on the ability and willingness to complete
the task, and often, the best routes to successfully completing it. In this
respect, the act of delegating work should be seen almost as a contract
where objectives, methods, budgets, resources and deadlines are all
openly discussed and agreed upon.

## 1.3    What delegation is not

Delegation means much more than simply dishing out orders to your
employees. We shall see in section 5 that the process of delegation, if well
executed, involves several factors.

Delegation, if properly done, is not abdication. A task well-delegated keeps you in control while giving the person delegated to the freedom and motivation to succeed and save you time. Some managers are apprehensive about handing over authority or wrongly believe they can produce better results on their own.

Effective delegation is not micromanagement, where a manager provides too much input, direction and review of delegated work. There can be a fine line between giving guidance to a team and being overbearing. Managers frequently believe they are helping their team perform by "keeping tabs" on work when sometimes they ought to give employees space to be creative, grow in confidence and hone their skills. Micromanagement reduces productivity, causes frustration, feeds arguments and lowers morale. Good delegation increases efficiency, boosts team confidence, supports personal growth and development and helps achieve quality results.

We will tackle these issues further on in this guidebook.

# 2. WHY DELEGATION IS SO IMPORTANT

## 2.1    Operational and business importance

One of the most fundamental tasks of management is to achieve results by sharing-out, structuring and coordinating the efforts of individual team members or entire teams.

Businesses cannot operate smoothly without effective delegation. Imagine every decision having to be referred upwards. Imagine also a company in which the management delegate everything without any control or minimal discussion and coordination.

Delegating consistently well – that's efficiently, effectively and economically – is a tremendous test of leadership and management skill. Well-executed it is undoubtedly a key ingredient of successful management performance, achieving great outcomes and sustainable results. It can be a source of competitive advantage too.

Delegation can improve responsiveness to customers and customer care. It is often counter-productive for a customer to wait for upward referrals within an organization. In an exceptional situation or complex transaction it may be necessary, but overwhelmingly, the people who have the customer-facing jobs have the most information about how best to serve the customer. So it is important to delegate and empower staff to take the actions necessary to provide the customer with the service and solutions they need, promptly and effectively.

## 2.2    It reflects who you are as a leader and strongly impacts your effectiveness

Delegating undoubtedly saves you precious time, that if used wisely, can improve your overall business performance. Depending on your priorities, you may have to delegate aspects that you could do better than anyone else but need to contribute in a different and less time-consuming way than doing the task alone.

It is also common for leaders and managers to neglect the longer or medium-term tasks that keep a business competitively positioned. Delegation can be key to ensuring managers have the time to spend on those strategic things that are very important but not urgent.

We all have the challenge to be efficient and effective in leveraging our own talents and to make the biggest difference we can in the time we allocate to our work. There are things that only we can do. It can be difficult at times to see our unique contribution. What is yours?

_____

_____

_____

_____

_____

_____

## 2.3    Importance to team members and individuals

Our teams and organizations have many individual talents that need to be utilized and developed. Additionally, clusters of diverse individual talents in teams and organizations can be powerful in creating differentials for the business.

Giving responsibilities to your subordinates shows you respect their talent and trust their judgment. When employees feel respected they tend to be more committed to the task, the company and you as a manager. By entrusting employees with decision-making authority they also tend to feel a greater sense of ownership of the work and ensure it is completed successfully.

By supplying your team with new challenges, you motivate them and stretch their skills.

## 2.4    Importance to succession management

You may not realize at first, but delegating well means you can move on to greater tasks and develop your own skills. Skill development will prepare you and your team for future tasks and roles within the company. This is exactly why effective delegation breeds sustainable and successful businesses. A good manager always develops talent within the company to take things forward when he/she progresses up the ladder. Often your superiors form strong impressions of how well you delegate and develop your team. It is common for them to look beyond the results and outcomes to whether the team is sustainable after you move on.

What would improving the one thing you answered in the previous section mean to you? How important would it be?

# 3. NOT ONLY IS IT IMPORTANT, IT'S CHALLENGING!

At times delegation can be very challenging to do well. It can involve the complexities of critical thinking, people and communication skills, and knowing what's important in driving results.

As work becomes more complex some of the boundaries between individuals and teams can be less clear and collaborative creation can play more of a part. How and when the manager involves others in collaborative activities is of importance.

Often the individuals or teams delegated to are under the manager's control. However, project work and matrix organizations increasingly require dividing tasks with people over whom one does not have line authority. Outsourcing, for instance, can be useful in obtaining a specific or expert contribution from a cost-effective external resource.

## 3.1 Common outcomes of good delegation

Which of these good outcomes have you experienced?

Yes    No

☐    ☐    Satisfaction in succeeding with a task or objective.

☐    ☐    Reinforcement of the confidence and trust in working relationships.

☐    ☐    Good reputation of the team and increasingly challenging and important work.

☐    ☐    Tasks completed well: fit for purpose and delivered on time, on budget and with the required quality.

☐    ☐    Personal and professional development and meeting career goals.

| Yes | No | |
|-----|-----|-----|
| ☐ | ☐ | A real contribution to making succession planning work in practice. |
| ☐ | ☐ | Contributions to good team morale and staff satisfaction. |
| ☐ | ☐ | Confidence in further delegation and succeeding in other tasks. |
| ☐ | ☐ | Willingness of staff to grow and seek further challenges. |
| ☐ | ☐ | There is adequate time and focus given to managing the future as well as today's urgent tasks. |

### 3.2 Common outcomes of bad delegation

These are the opposite of the positive outcomes. Have you experienced any?

| Yes | No | |
|-----|-----|-----|
| ☐ | ☐ | Failure to achieve the task or purpose itself through missed deadlines, budgets or quality of functionality. |
| ☐ | ☐ | Frustration. |
| ☐ | ☐ | Demotivated staff. |
| ☐ | ☐ | Deterioration in trust, confidence and relationships. |
| ☐ | ☐ | Confusion. |
| ☐ | ☐ | Fears of further delegation. |
| ☐ | ☐ | Uneven sharing of working hours – a few working much more than others. |

# 4. DIMENSIONS OF DELEGATION

The following dimensions of delegation help us think more broadly about the subject and our preferences, before we look in more detail at the delegation process.

## 4.1    Sources of delegated work

Think of your work as a system. Some of this will be "steady state" (routine or standard work that is ongoing and central to your purpose) and some will relate to new projects and new tasks.

Where do these new tasks come from? Are they from:

• Your boss.
• Another superior or the board if you are a CEO.
• Your customers.
• Other areas in your organization.
• New ideas from within the team.
• Your own initiative.
• Changes in the marketplace.
• Changes in technology.
• Competitor analysis.
• Agreed strategic or operational plans.

Reflect on the sources in your area. What does the mix say about the nature of your work and whether you are able to control the mix with the purpose of making the most difference?

_____

_____

_____

Are there repetitive emergencies or urgent tasks that require you or the business to come up with better controls, procedures or systems?

_____

_____

_____

## 4.2     Types of tasks or objectives that can be delegated

We can delegate:

* Routine tasks.
* Broad or narrow objectives and goals.
* Controls.
* Generation of ideas and strategies.
* Research, gathering opinions or inputs to decisions.
* Development of an innovation or new procedure.
* Decisions.
* Projects – parts or in their entirety.
* Responsibility to achieve results and outcomes.

Think about your work. What types of tasks or objectives do you most and least delegate?

_____

_____

_____

_____

_____

_____

Is something out of balance?

Yes/No _____

_____

_____

Does it reflect a concern or difficulty you have?

Yes/No _____

_____

_____

## 4.3    Who you might delegate to

We can delegate to:

- Our direct reports – i.e., Those individually under our direct hierarchical management control. We ideally have a good mix of talents and experience in our team and we need to know the strengths and areas of development of each member.

- A team under our control – We might nominate a team head who we will hold accountable, or in some circumstances we may delegate that nomination to the team. The team may have different coordinators for different aspects.

- Peers or internal partners – This may require negotiation and exchange as we do not have direct authority in this case. Sometimes it may be agreed by a person or people who have authority over both you and your peer.

- Our boss or superior – Sometimes we may need to consult our superior and "delegate upwards." This is discussed more in section 5.4. Sometimes due to resource or priority restrictions, or a task being better done elsewhere, we may need the support of our boss to reallocate or "re-prioritize" a task.

- Outsourced resources – Sometimes due to lack of resources, capacity or skills a task/objective that truly belongs to our area may need to be supported or completed by an outsource's resource. We will probably need the budget to do this. The decision-making on whether to staff or outsource can depend on several factors.

What is your world of delegation like? What mix of the above forms your everyday delegation of tasks?

_____

_____

_____

_____

_____

What improvements or reallocations could you make?

_____

_____

_____

Can other staff members better support you in keeping control over delegated work?

_____

_____

_____

Can you improve the capability or capacity of the employees you delegate to? If so, what actions would make the biggest difference?

_____

_____

_____

## 4.4    Levels of capability and motivation – styles of delegation

As a manager you are likely to have a mix of qualities and development needs in your staff. This diversity has advantages but extremes can cause serious difficulties. For example, too many inexperienced staff may require you to spend too much time directing and supporting staff. On the other hand, a team that has been doing much the same thing for a long time and needs little support or coaching can lack motivation. We often see in sports teams how a mix of experience and youth can provide spark, learning and energy.

Think about how you should vary your delegation style and process in the following cases if one of your staff:

a.   Has the skills, confidence and will to do the task in hand.

_____

_____

_____

b.  Has the necessary skills but lacks some confidence or motivation to execute the task to the best of their ability.

_____

_____

_____

c.  Lacks skills to execute the task and wants to do it but believes, sometimes falsely, that they can do it.

_____

_____

_____

d.  Has several necessary skills, but lacks some others to execute the task and consequently lacks confidence.

_____

_____

_____

Remember that you need to be as transparent as possible in discussing, negotiating and agreeing with the staff member what style of delegation is most appropriate.

For type a: You might wish to delegate with some extra challenge to see if this confident individual can grow. Your checkpoints and support may be less frequent. You may agree some parameters in which the person will let you know early if the task is facing difficulties.

For type b: You may need to agree ways that will support the individual in areas where confidence or motivation is difficult.

For type c: You may wish to leverage their motivation but coach them through the area of skill deficit. Alternatively, you may get someone with the necessary skills to coach them.

For type d: You may need to take a closer hands-on role in supporting and directing them through the task. Is it one that they can do themselves after one experience? Should it be broken down into learnable pieces?

## 4.5    Levels of responsibility and authority

Delegation can vary in the levels of responsibility you entrust to an employee and doesn't always require that full authority over a task be passed on. However, delegation requires that you give a subordinate a level of discretion that sometimes isn't present in their role. This means the authority to make decisions that formally belong to your position, but for which you are still accountable.

As an example, a retail manager may give an employee responsibility over computer sales without giving him/her the authority to give discounts, take cash payments or accept returns and make refunds. The manager then acts as a supervisor during the computer sales assignment. At one extreme the manager might help execute every sale, take every payment and observe every other move made by the employee. The other extreme would be that of "empowerment" whereby a delegator entrusts full authority and full responsibility for achieving goals, executing the task and the final results.

How much control over an assignment is given depends on various factors such as employee experience, reliability on previous assignments and the magnitude and complexity of the task. Empowered employees are given scope to manage aspects such as innovation and customer service without the intervention of others. There can also be internal controls that operate to ensure that no one is unnecessarily exposed to temptation or opportunity to defraud the organization.

One of the key dimensions of business is the "trust-control dilemma" (Handy, 1993). Trust helps develop people and their motivation while control costs time and money. Control is an essential element of the sustainability of a business. Managing this dilemma can require great skill and judgment.

### Levels of authority and delegation

To get an even greater understanding of the levels of delegation possible we can look at examples of instructions bosses can give employees.

a.  "This is the way I want you to do this," or "I'll let you know exactly what you'll have to do."

At this extreme a manager is telling an employee what to do and how to complete a task. At this level there is no freedom. The boss has a strong involvement in the task, which can use up a lot of his/her time.

b.  "Can you please do some research on this topic and get back to me so that I can decide what to do."

There is a little more input and analysis from the employee at this level but the decision is ultimately the boss's.

c.  "Do some research for me on this topic and we'll discuss it together."

A step up from the previous example, the boss wants the employee's opinion and is willing to discuss it and come up with a mutual final decision.

d.  "I want your analysis and decision on the situation and I'll give you the heads up."

Here the boss will begin allowing the employee to make decisions but wants to check the rationale before giving their approval.

e.  "Make your decision and go ahead with it unless I tell you otherwise."

Here the employee is making the decision and the boss is only requesting a little information to quickly judge whether they disapprove. This gives the employee a lot of power but in the rare event the boss has to intervene, he/she has the ability to do so.

f.  "Make the decision and go ahead with it. Tell me later how it went."

In this example the employee already has the green light. Only after the fact will the boss ask questions. Clearly at this level there is a lot of trust in the employee's ability to decide and carry out the task to a satisfactory standard.

g.  "You decide and implement your decision. If anything comes up you should be able to manage things. I'm entrusting you with this area of the business. No need for my involvement."

This is an example of empowerment discussed earlier. The employee is in full control of the decision, process and managing the outcomes. The boss doesn't intend to provide any input of ideas or manage any eventuality. That is completely up to the respected and trusted employee. At this extreme the boss saves a lot of their valuable time, but possibly at the expense of the quality of results, depending on the employee they delegated to.

## 4.6    The trust and control spectrum

Good internal controls can help avoid catastrophic or expensive fraudulent abuses. Bad internal control can stifle creativity, create an atmosphere of fear and the lack of motivation to take the risks that sometimes benefit the business greatly.

The same can apply to your delegation.

How well do you balance the trust and control dilemma? What do others say?

_____

_____

_____

In what ways can you control tasks more effectively and efficiently? What creative techniques could you employ here?

_____

_____

_____

_____

As a general rule it is very important to try to balance levels of responsibility and authority. Having full responsibility for a result or outcome, but lack authority to approve key ingredients to achieving a result can be a source of demotivation or conflict.

Later on we'll look at how best to concede control to employees and how trusting you are as a manager.

## 4.7    Delegation and seniority

The style and nature of delegation can change as you go higher in an organization. At lower supervisory levels delegation can be more task and operationally driven. As you rise up the organization the mix can change to be less task driven and more objective driven. More of your time may go into finding and prioritizing the right objectives and strategies to ensure sustainable success. You may find yourself delegating whole strategic objectives to a senior executive who has the experience and team to deliver on the challenge.

A promotion can be a challenge in relation to your delegation. You may have become comfortable in the decisions and activities in your previous role. Transitioning may mean you need to "step-out" of the old role, perhaps mentoring your successor, but not interfering, whilst you concentrate on fully assuming your new role and challenge.

## 4.8    Risk

Not only is there the aspect of the trust-control dilemma, but there can be other aspects of risk involved in a delegated task.

Other aspects of risk that may affect the frequency of your informal and formal controls over delegated work can be:

- The criticality of the task to your future and reputation.
- The criticality of the task to your team's reputation.
- The criticality of the task to your organization's reputation if it were to go wrong.
- The relative profit and loss impacts if the task is well or poorly done.
- The complexity and inherent risk within the task.

As previously with the trust-control dilemma, risk requires mature judgment. Overreacting and "over-controlling" can put the task itself at risk. Lack of consideration of risk can lead to unnecessary losses or surprises.

Another way of looking at this is that mistakes are always possible. Some mistakes have a good return on them in terms of learning. Others are clearly "too expensive." Sometimes totally unexpected things can happen that could not have been foreseen even by diligent risk management. We all know that it's really important to learn from our mistakes and to be diligent in not repeating them.

Which of your delegated tasks or projects have the highest risk profile?

_____

_____

_____

_____

What could you do better in terms of mitigating those risks on a more effective, economic or efficient basis?

_____

_____

_____

_____

# 5. "B" AND BEST PRACTICE

## 5.1  A process for delegating a new task

The flowchart model of the delegation process is designed to be relatively comprehensive. It can be used for simple as well as more complex tasks. For simple or routine tasks you may be able to simplify some of the steps or consolidate them over a series of delegated tasks. Regardless, knowing the principles behind this process will stand you in good stead.

*Delegation flowchart\**

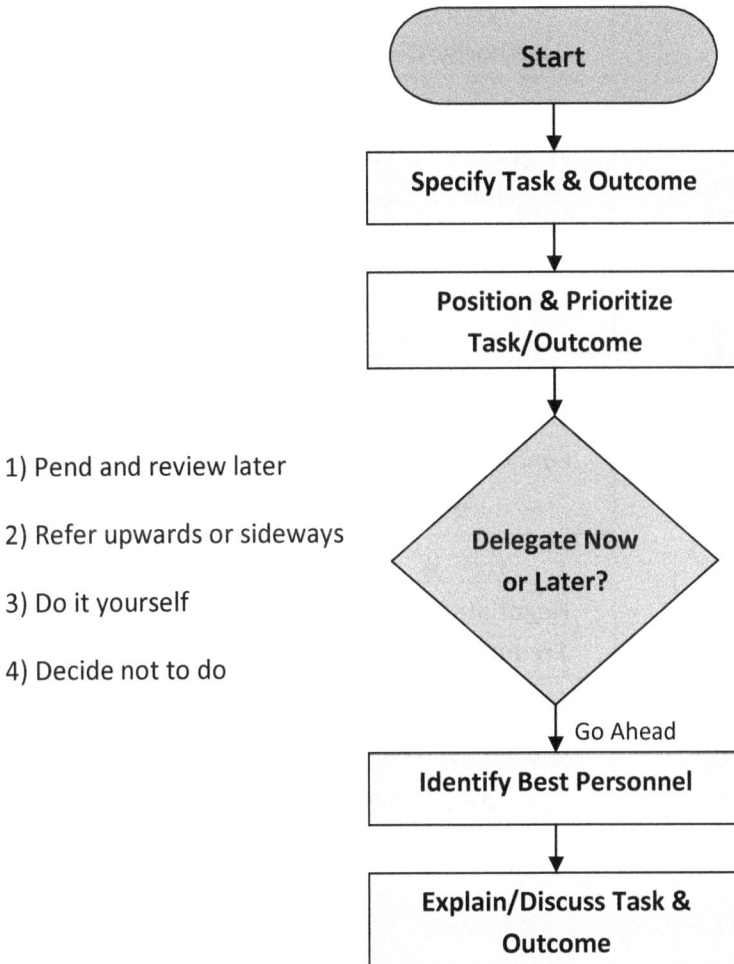

1) Pend and review later

2) Refer upwards or sideways

3) Do it yourself

4) Decide not to do

```
                    ┌─────────────┐
                    │    Start    │
                    └─────────────┘
                           │
                    ┌─────────────────────┐
                    │ Specify Task & Outcome │
                    └─────────────────────┘
                           │
                    ┌─────────────────────┐
                    │ Position & Prioritize │
                    │    Task/Outcome      │
                    └─────────────────────┘
                           │
                    ◇ Delegate Now or Later? ◇
                           │ Go Ahead
                    ┌─────────────────────┐
                    │ Identify Best Personnel │
                    └─────────────────────┘
                           │
                    ┌─────────────────────┐
                    │ Explain/Discuss Task & │
                    │       Outcome        │
                    └─────────────────────┘
```

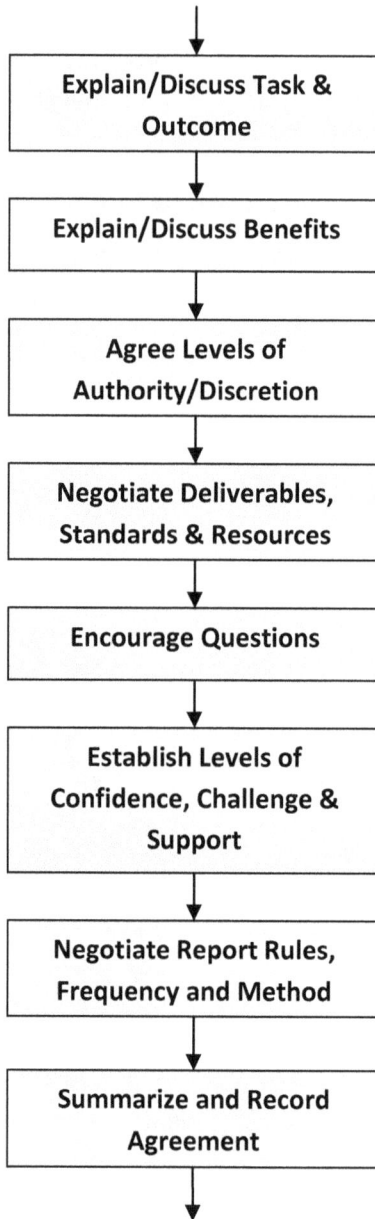

```
              │
              ▼
┌─────────────────────────────┐
│   Explain/Discuss Task &    │
│          Outcome            │
└─────────────────────────────┘
              │
              ▼
┌─────────────────────────────┐
│   Explain/Discuss Benefits  │
└─────────────────────────────┘
              │
              ▼
┌─────────────────────────────┐
│        Agree Levels of      │
│     Authority/Discretion    │
└─────────────────────────────┘
              │
              ▼
┌─────────────────────────────┐
│   Negotiate Deliverables,   │
│    Standards & Resources    │
└─────────────────────────────┘
              │
              ▼
┌─────────────────────────────┐
│     Encourage Questions     │
└─────────────────────────────┘
              │
              ▼
┌─────────────────────────────┐
│     Establish Levels of     │
│   Confidence, Challenge &   │
│           Support           │
└─────────────────────────────┘
              │
              ▼
┌─────────────────────────────┐
│   Negotiate Report Rules,   │
│    Frequency and Method     │
└─────────────────────────────┘
              │
              ▼
┌─────────────────────────────┐
│    Summarize and Record     │
│          Agreement          │
└─────────────────────────────┘
              │
              ▼
```

```
              ┌─────────────────────────┐
         ┌───▶│   Diarize Checkpoints   │
         │    └─────────────────────────┘
         │                 │
         │                 ▼
         │            ╱─────────╲
         │          ╱             ╲
  Agree Next Review│  Periodic Status │
         └─────────┤     Checks       │
                    ╲             ╱
                      ╲─────────╱
                           │  Completion
                           ▼
              ┌─────────────────────────┐
              │  Completed Task/Outcome │
              └─────────────────────────┘
                           │
                           ▼
              ┌─────────────────────────┐
              │    Evaluate Outcomes    │
              │     (Post-mortem)       │
              └─────────────────────────┘
                           │
                           ▼
              ┌─────────────────────────┐
              │      Seek Feedback      │
              └─────────────────────────┘
                           │
                           ▼
              ┌─────────────────────────┐
              │      Give Feedback      │
              └─────────────────────────┘
                           │
                           ▼
              ┌─────────────────────────┐
              │    Prioritize/Agree     │
              │    Recommendations      │
              └─────────────────────────┘
                           │
                           ▼
                    (      End      )
```

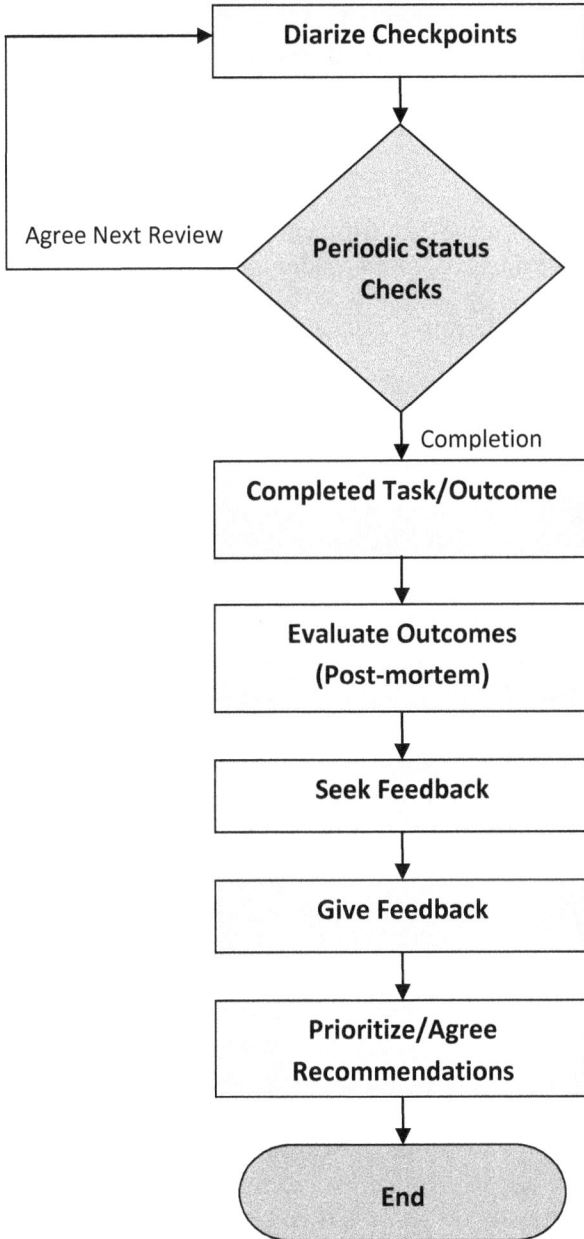

\*Printable version available on www.thrive-careers.com

Here is the thinking behind each step:

### Step 1. Specify task & outcome –

Determine what needs to be completed and the result you want to achieve from the task. Specify outcomes as clearly and as comprehensively as necessary. This may include some or all of:

- The result.
- What the result looks like from certain key perspectives: i.e., The user, the customer, the shareholder etc.
- The cost(s).
- The quality or reliability required.
- The acceptable time frames.

### Step 2. Position & prioritize task / outcome –

Here you evaluate the task based on type, fit, skills required, risk and priority to help you in the steps to follow.

Where does the outcome expressed in Step 1 come in your consideration of priorities (for useful tools here refer to the *A to B Guide to Prioritization*)? What is the value added by this outcome? Is it a key step in achieving or facilitating other things? How well does it compare to other priorities? Is there enough energy and focus for this task? Could it potentially distract the organization from other core goals? On a scale how would this task rank on the list of priorities? Is it important in terms of short, medium or long term priorities?

Determine what type of task or challenge you are dealing with here. Is it a routine spreadsheet setup, new concept pitch, sales/manufacturing target or cost/efficiency enhancement goal? Every task presents different sets of challenges, requires different talents and possibly different team dynamics.

Next is to observe whether the new task fits with what you and the organization are already doing. Would the task slot in nicely with what employees are already doing or is this completely new territory for the organization? Does it require a typical or unusual combination of skills that will require a number of skilled individuals to collaborate? Based on this assessment you may later decide to go ahead, scrap the task or complete it at a later date when there is a better "fit." Assessing the fit also helps managers detect potential needs for additional resources, be it a new employee, better software or more capital resources.

Without choosing a person or a team to complete the task just yet, figure out what core skills are required for this task. Does the person need to be able to persuade a new client, analyze data or have experience leading change? Stepping back and looking first for skills, rather than people, will help you position the task better.

Is the task high, medium or low-risk? Is your organization ready to take on the level of risk present in the task should it not succeed? Does the task have the potential to affect your career within the organization? This brief risk assessment will help you decide on whether the task is essential and plausible, whether the complexity and risk make it worth progressing or a new approach is needed that mitigates the risks and simplifies the challenge.

### *Step 3. Delegate the task now or later? –*

Based on the positioning and prioritization exercise in the previous step, decide whether to delegate the task now, at a specific later time, not at all or to hold off the task with a specific review date.

For example, if perhaps you and your subordinates are too busy or have more pressing matters to take care of you may choose to hold off the project and review at a later date. Maybe the task requires training for which there isn't enough time just yet.

Depending on the task you may feel you lack the political influence to move it forward and hence you need to refer the task upwards.

Perhaps the task is better done in another area and your relationship with the peer who runs that area is constructive and mutually supportive and you can readily get your peer to take it on. Perhaps you might need some support from your boss or a superior to do this if it is likely to be met with resistance. If so, it might indicate you can usefully build a more mutually interdependent relationship with the peer involved.

Ask yourself if there is essential expertise needed to complete the task and whether you can pass this expertise onto others. Is it critical that you do it yourself? If employees lack certain skills, would the task give them an opportunity to grow without posing major risks to the organization? Occasionally, you may prefer to complete a task by yourself if you believe your subordinates lack crucial skills. You also may want to ask yourself if the task will have to be repeated in future and you therefore should begin training staff members.

There are also times when you may want to scrap a task altogether. It might be, for example, that it is a proposal for an improved IT system that will deliver efficiency and control savings. However, you assess that the project's complexity is such that it will tie up too many key personnel who are already focused on projects with similar gains but less risk. The IT strategy is looking at an entirely new platform in eighteen months time and you decide to scrap the project in light of this likely broader overhaul of the IT systems.

*Step 4. Identify the best personnel –*

Finding the ideal person(s) to carry out a task isn't always as simple as it may sound. It can require a keen eye for people's talents, their ability to adapt and work within a team. When selecting the right personnel it also requires a level of trust. You may feel like you are "letting go" but you shouldn't feel as though you've just put all your money on number 35. If so, you have probably chosen the wrong person(s).

If your team members have more experience than you in a certain task you should not be reticent. Know what value you can add. Perhaps this will be through prioritizing, aligning tasks, motivating, asking challenging questions, ensuring resources are made available, overcoming political barriers etc. Management and leadership involve much more than technical expertise.

Try to distribute mundane tasks fairly amongst your team members and ensure you have your fair share! The same can apply to the exciting and interesting tasks.

*Step 5. Explain/discuss task & outcome –*

Once you've picked the right person for the task you must explain clearly what it is you need them to do and what you want them to achieve. Remember, clear communication is essential. Check for understanding by asking open questions. Go over why you selected the assumptions and conclusions you have made in all the previous steps. Ask for their views.

Possible questions might be: "How feasible do you think this is?", "What are the alternative ways to achieve the result?", "What are the most difficult challenges?" Look for signs of enthusiasm or reluctance. If you see either, ask about how they feel about the task. Is their answer congruent with their tone of voice or body language?

*Step 6. Explain/discuss benefits –*

Part of understanding what is required from a task comes from discussing not just the required result, but also how the task adds value to the organization and benefits the individuals executing it. Help employees visualize the effect a positive outcome will have on the organization and the individual's personal development. This will help motivate them, instill a sense of ownership and help them understand the purpose of the task. With a clear purpose individuals know where they are heading and why they are heading there!

Again, check for understanding with open questions. Ask, if appropriate, if they can envisage any other benefits and whether it is an exciting challenge.

*Step 7. Agree levels of authority/discretion –*

If you skip this stage you may end up biting your toes later. Agreeing levels of authority ensures you only allow as much discretion as necessary, shows respect for the delegate and makes the boundaries clear. People otherwise may assume they have a level of authority beyond what you see fit and begin making decisions that can compromise the outcome without conferring with you.

Think carefully about authority levels and whether your decision would be considered abnormal or exceptional. This is a good area to review periodically or at the end of a delegated task or project, based on experience and outcomes.

*Step 8. Negotiate deliverables, standards and the resources –*

By openly discussing the task, deadlines and quality standards you expect, you can gauge someone's reaction and negotiate these key elements. In negotiating deliverables you increase the likelihood the task will meet its criteria and that the employee feels comfortable to execute.

An employee used to dealing with $100,000 contracts with small suppliers may feel incapable of negotiating $1m contracts with larger firms. Similarly, a hefty task with a short deadline and an ultra-conservative budget won't give your staff much enthusiasm to achieve.

When an employee agrees to complete a task and is happy with the responsibility and comfortable with the time-scale and other working parameters results are often faster and better.

If there is no agreement in the first place a project is bound to stumble on a few rocks as people have different expectations, work styles, skills and fears. Often when there is no accord at the beginning, employees return to your desk on the deadline with a half-baked piece of work that may not even satisfy your objectives.

There may be resources and cooperation needed to meet the objective. The support levels and resources need to be carefully negotiated. These can include budget, materials, technology, process, software, permanent or temporary staff with the right skills, location or space etc. Support can include things like training, mentoring, coaching and on-going feedback.

### Step 9. Encourage questions –

This is about getting employees to express areas of concern and ensure they fully understand what is expected of them with regards to the task. Whether it is a question about the final picture or the small details needed to get there, solving those before they begin work will save you and them valuable time. Too often managers give orders and ship off employees full of question marks in their heads to later find the work isn't up to scratch. Don't assume that the employee is clear and happy about everything – ask if there is anything else they need to know. Do they have any further doubts or concerns? Often you will know if you have encouraged a good dialogue – is the employee asking insightful questions?

Open communication is essential to ensuring objectives are met, work delivered on time and staff are motivated and comfortable with their responsibilities.

Wouldn't it be better for staff to come back to you to discuss a small hic-cup and ask for advice instead of causing an even greater disaster out of fear or reluctance to talk to you?

### Step 10. Establish levels of confidence, challenge and support –

This step is a final check that all the parties have adequately discussed the key challenges in the task and the support that the employee will need to succeed and feel confident to proceed.

### Step 11. Negotiate report rules, frequency and method –

Maybe, for example, you'd like to receive a weekly copy of the current sales figures or get periodical updates on the evolution of a project. Now is the time to specify what you'd like to be reported on, how often and how. This will keep you updated without being overbearing and keep employees en route to successfully completing the task.

You should also be clear about the circumstances in which you need an immediate alert or an exceptional report. It's best to know early if things are going off-track or if there are surprises.

You should be clear about what reporting needs to be formal and in writing and what can be verbal or informal. You may wish to incorporate updates into the agenda of regular meetings.

### Step 12. Summarize and record agreement –

Reinforce the main points and record agreed periodic status checks and end results. The point of this is that people cannot be held accountable for something they haven't committed to. If they have gone through this contracting process they will inevitably show more commitment. For less important tasks or simpler tasks the agreement can be verbal. At the end of the conversation it's good to get the employee in question to record or state the agreement. This is a way of ensuring full understanding.

### Step 13. Diarize checkpoints –

Should you feel necessary to have your own controls that key reporting deadlines are met then enter the checkpoints in your agenda or project control log.

Often a task is critical to the objectives set out for your role within an organization and demands your own controls and checks. High-risk and high-profile tasks can't be entirely delegated and reliant on occasional informal status checks.

Whilst you are waiting for a key report you might wish to visit the site of the project to talk to people or visit the people affected by the work. For example, if you are awaiting the sales figures and consumer reports on your latest product you may want to pay visits to suppliers, manufacturers and retailers to see if everything is running smoothly.

Depending on the task and the reliability of the staff you've appointed, your personal checks won't need to be as frequent or widespread. But letting go of your own control system altogether can hurt you and the organization should things start going the wrong way.

### Step 14. Periodic status checks –

This serves to evaluate progress, make tweaks, give advice and support. Agree further reviews until the task is fully completed.

### Step 15. Completed task / outcome –

The task may be finished but delegation doesn't always end here…

### Step 16. Evaluate outcomes (post-mortem) –

Analyze the final result. Is it truly complete? Has it met the criteria you first set out earlier? Has the task been fully delivered and verified as working to specifications? What were the final costs, time frames and quality or functionality? Did it surpass expectations?

### Step 17. Seek feedback –

Find out how you did as a delegator. Do your employees feel you were clear in your objectives? Did you make them feel comfortable enough to ask questions and seek advice? Do they feel you were overbearing at any point? Were there any lessons that can be learned from surprises (positive or negative) or variances in the final outcome against original plans and specifications?

*Step 18. Give feedback –*

Let your employees know how they did at each step of the way to the finish line. Tell them what your observations were on the task itself and their personal progress. Be objective and supportive.

*Step 19. Praise / agree recommendations –*

Praise your employees where praise is due and constructively criticize what could have been done better. Always give feedback and recommendations. It allows employees to make improvements and feel appreciated.

As a general principle give feedback promptly when something deserves praise or thanks, or alternatively, needs addressing or correcting.

If things go wrong, be honest about it if your delegation decisions turned out to be inappropriate. Assume your proper responsibility as a manager. Excuse innocent mistakes the first time – ask what the person has learned and how they hope to avoid the same mistake again. Be assertive in dealing with unacceptable behavior but only once you have asked the other person involved for their viewpoint and are certain of their misconduct.

## 5.2    Knowing when and how to step in or step out

It's useful and important to have a good process in mind, but you also have to exercise judgment and flexibility in leading and managing people. Even if things are going well you can "step in." Think about acknowledging progress and spreading the news as appropriate without exaggerating or pre-empting expectations. Think about how you can continue to leverage the things your team members have shown real strengths in. Protect the team from things that could unnecessarily disturb their successful rhythm.

Also be clear about how and when to "step out." Encourage people to be responsible and self-managing as far as possible. Build trust and their understanding of when and how to report to you on exceptions or doubts. Sometimes they might only need a minute of your time but that one doubt may be really important. Don't let staff put the "monkey on your back" when it's not right to do so. Ensure that you have an atmosphere in which good simple open questions are encouraged and used by yourself and all the team.

When things are not going well, step in as the captain of a ship would do. Understand the problem, its route causes, what has and has not been tried and what has worked in the past. Ask challenging questions, leverage the talents of the team and make the decision to get back on track.

## 5.3    Managing portfolios of delegated tasks

The previous sections set out a detailed process to manage a delegated task. However, you also need to know about how to manage "portfolios" of tasks.

When you think about the delegation that is already in place in your area you will see that each individual has a stock of tasks (perhaps of differing types as in section 4.2).

It is useful to think of these portfolios as activities in themselves:

- What are the commonalities and diversities involved?

- What skills are required?

- What aspects are missing or rare? – The opportunity to be creative? Strategic work?

For each individual it is important to discuss and have a developmental or improvement plan for each of the aspects as necessary:

- What are the individual's strengths and development needs?

- What is the mix of tasks like?

- What is the mix of routine and "non-routine" tasks?

- How many hours is the individual working and what does time analysis show?

- How efficient and effective is the individual in delivering on each major type of task?

- What new or extended types of tasks is the individual ready to assume?

- What types of tasks does the individual need training to assume?

Then looking at the team as a whole:

- What reallocation of tasks would be beneficial in developing staff and motivation?

- What is the equity or the division of portfolios?

- What team talents could be better leveraged?

Use the space below to write any notes:

_____

_____

_____

_____

An analysis of your personal and team's time management can be very revealing. Here we have a useful matrix for managing your time effectively.

Create a 2 x 2 matrix of:

| Important | Not Important |
|-----------|---------------|
| Urgent    | Not Urgent    |

(Stephen Covey, *The Seven Habits of Highly Effective People*)

Estimate what percentage of your time and your team's time goes into each box. Brainstorm about how you can make improvements to your delegation. It is very common that the urgent eats up the not-urgent but important. Unimportant things clearly need to be kept to a minimum.

What are the key aspects and issues arising from your "portfolio" and time management reviews?

_____

_____

_____

_____

## 5.4    Bosses and delegating upwards

There will be times when you have to delegate tasks to your boss – this isn't always easy. The *A to B Guide to Dealing with Difficult Bosses* goes into more detail on the many aspects of working well with your boss. Here we'll focus on delegating to them.

Ideally you have a "win-win-win" relationship with your boss: he or she helps you and your unit be successful, you help your boss be successful and together you help the organization succeed.

It takes time and effort to understand and negotiate in detail what "win-win-win" means and how best to deal with opportunities and threats, leverage strengths and improve on material weaknesses.

There may be times your boss does not delegate to you appropriately. Perhaps he/she has his/her own limitations with respect to the best practice set out in this guidebook. If you know the success your boss is looking for, how he or she prefers to work and communicate and you have built a good relationship, you are in a better position to discuss conflicts that are caused by his/her delegation style.

There are occasions within an organization when a task requires greater expertise, additional resources or political influence. To overcome such barriers you may need the help of your superior who has the authority, technical knowledge or management experience that you may not yet have.

Having authority within an organization can make giving orders easier since subordinates feel an obligation to comply, though as we've discussed, may not be motivated to do so. When delegating upwards, however, matters aren't so easy. You know you need the assistance of your superior but you don't want to appear incompetent, come across in the wrong light or give the impression you'd rather be managing him/her.

The key is to understand and motivate your boss, be confident and persuasive in your approach and work on the way you project yourself.

Write down the key challenges arising from the way your boss delegates to you:

_____

_____

_____

_____

_____

Write down the three main things that motivate your boss:

1)_____

2)_____

3)_____

Don't know? Try to find out by asking others who report to him/her...

What ideas do you have to build your confidence and persuasion for dealing with your boss? Do they fit well with what motivates him or her?

_____

_____

_____

Can you improve the way you project yourself, your tone and positive attitude in your dealings with your boss? Write your ideas here.

_____

_____

_____

_____

Here are common workplace situations where delegating upwards is necessary and how best to tackle them:

- *You have a lot to do but can't possibly complete it all* – Analyze what compromises and adjustments you can make. Prioritize based upon sensible criteria (see *A to B Guide to Prioritization* for more information). Know what additional resources would make the most difference and think about the constraints and motivations of your boss. Be ready to explain, answer questions and jointly create the best solutions with your boss.

- *You lack political clout to complete a task* – You have maximized your influence and power base (see the *A to B Guide to Office Politics* for more information), but the political dynamics mean you need your boss's support. Your boss is likely to support you if the objective is aligned with his or her objectives and is willing to use political capital to make it happen.

- *Your boss has a lot more expertise than you on a specific task or challenge, but you don't want to appear incompetent* – You can think positively and tell your boss what you bring to the table and ask questions on how to bridge the gap in your expertise.

- *Your boss is willing to help, but is very busy also* – You will need to ensure you have a mutual way of prioritizing what is most important and what alternatives you both have. Ask good open questions about relative importance/priorities, options, perceived barriers, how your area can support your boss and vice versa.

Ask yourself:

Does my boss delegate too much or too little to me?

_____

_____

Are there parts of my job that my boss could better support me on?

_____

_____

_____

Does my boss help me get my budget and resources right to deliver the required results?

_____

_____

Can I support my boss better in achieving any of his/her responsibilities? How can I do this?

_____

_____

_____

_____

Are there steps of the delegation process my boss needs to improve on? Which ones?

_____

_____

_____

_____

If my boss wants to delegate something to me that I believe is better done elsewhere will he or she listen and fairly consider my point?

_____

_____

Does my boss support me with the training and mentoring I need to progress and deliver?

_____

_____

_____

Is it clear when I must report to my boss on progress or exceptions?

_____

_____

## 5.5    Outsourcing decisions

Outsourcing can be complex and these thoughts are only intended to help you make an initial assessment. The main considerations in determining whether or not to outsource are as follows:

- Is this task or project something that can be delivered either better, faster or at a lower cost than you can do in-house?

- What is strategically or operationally important in deciding which factors are pivotal?

- What are the barriers to delivering the same in-house?

- Are there alternatives or options to adequately diminish or overcome such barriers?

- What are the risk factors involved in the main in-house or outsourced options?

- How can we contractually mitigate the economic risks and costs if outsourcing delivery is delayed or fails?

- Does it make sense to pay a success fee component?

- What is the risk of the supplier having economic or resourcing problems during the term of the contract?

- What is the independently verifiable record of delivery of the supplier?

- What do we gain and lose from outsourcing?

- Is the task central to our strategy and business differentiation – should we bring it in-house?

- What restrictions are there on learning from and applying the intellectual property of the supplier if we later chose to bring the activity in-house?

# 6. YOUR "A"

We all have unique circumstances, a unique **A**. We each have our own experiences, talents, strengths, development needs as well as our own unique responsibilities within our organization.

## 6.1 What's working well?

"What's wrong?" or "What could be better?" are important questions, but it is better to start with the positive and to build on that foundation. This is a natural extension of human nature inherent in growing fields such as positive psychology and appreciative inquiry.

Use the structure of the guidebook to state what aspects of your delegation are working well. Later, review your answers to the sections on outcomes, dimensions and processes and other best practices.

Write down what has resonated with you as most worthy and valuable for your delegation in this guidebook so far:

_____

_____

_____

_____

_____

_____

_____

_____

How can you better leverage these aspects of your delegation?

_____

_____

_____

_____

## 6.2    What are your strengths?

Have you had the results of a 360 degree management/leadership instrument or questionnaire? What do they show? What have past results on management/leadership questionnaires said about you?

_____

_____

_____

_____

What positive verbal or written feedback have you had from your boss, direct reports, peers and internal or external customers on your personal performance?

_____

_____

_____

_____

Have you taken a strengths test? For instance, VIA or Gallup? If yes, what does this show?

_____

_____

_____

What would you add from your own self-knowledge as your proven strengths?

_____

_____

_____

_____

Later in section 7 you can think about how to leverage your strengths further, without overplaying them. You might also use them to work on your developmental areas.

Give yourself a pat on the back for the strengths you have developed and the credit you deserve for what is working well.

## 6.3    What could be better?

a.    Objective clues

Firstly, let's look for some objective clues as to what could be improved in your delegation. For this purpose, objective clues are firm observable facts or firm opinions of others.

In your answers list the key areas for improvement that are based on solid evidence in section 3 on the good and bad outcomes that can arise from delegation practices. For example, highly uneven work hours amongst different members of the team may indicate issues with your delegation or the need to train or coach some individuals.

List the objective clues you've found so far:

_____

_____

_____

_____

_____

_____

_____

b.    A closer look at you and your circumstances

Answer the following to help you look for more personal clues about your delegation:

Do you feel you have so much on your plate that you cannot organize yourself well enough?

_____

_____

_____

Are you working significantly different hours to others?

_____

_____

Are you frequently taking work home or working weekends while others are not?

_____

_____

Are staff asking you too frequently or not enough about their work?

_____

_____

How effectively does your area work when you are away or on vacation?

_____

_____

_____

Do you believe your subordinates come to you too often or too little to ask and check with you about the work delegated to them?

_____

_____

Do you feel you have to check others' work too often, or do you not have the time to check-up and support enough?

_____

_____

_____

Do you think you are neglecting important longer-term objectives because too much of your time goes into urgent business and activity?

_____

_____

How does your staff rate your delegation? Have you asked?

_____

_____

_____

From these answers you might want to add some notes on what else is going well or note some clear indicators of what you may need to improve:

_____

_____

_____

_____

c.   Delving deeper – knowing yourself and your role

To understand what kinds of tasks you probably should be delegating you need to know yourself and your role.

Think about your talents, experience, knowledge, relationships, access to resources and your role. What can only you do?

_____

_____

_____

This is often a key question as we take on more senior roles. When we transition to a senior role we may have a team of capable managers and implementers in our team. In this case, knowing the things that only we can do can help focus our role, as well as ensuring we delegate adequately and really transition into the executive role.

Do you truly know what is expected of you and what will define your success?

_____

_____

_____

Have you gone beyond your job description in discussing with your boss how he or she envisages success in your area and what the challenges and opportunities are?

_____

_____

_____

What are your key or non-negotiable priorities?

_____

_____

_____

What do you personally need to stop doing, keep doing, do more of and do less of?

_____

_____

_____

_____

How do a) your boss, b) your direct reports, c) your colleagues/peers and d) your internal and/or external customers answer the previous question?

_____

_____

_____

_____

_____

_____

_____

_____

What motivates you?

_____

_____

_____

_____

_____

_____

What has helped you change and grow in the past? Do you need to be applying some of those factors now?

_____

_____

_____

Make a summary from these questions and list:

The key strengths and resources you can leverage in your development:

_____

_____

_____

_____

_____

_____

Aspects that you need to take to your development plan:

_____

_____

_____

_____

_____

_____

Now check the relevant boxes based on your response to the following questions/statements. "Not at all" = 1, "Little" = 2, "Somewhat" = 3, "Very" = 4 and "Completely" = 5:

| | 1 | 2 | 3 | 4 | 5 |
|---|---|---|---|---|---|
| Am I a risk taker? | ☐ | ☐ | ☐ | ☐ | ☐ |
| Do I trust others? | ☐ | ☐ | ☐ | ☐ | ☐ |
| Can I let go of tasks I like doing? | ☐ | ☐ | ☐ | ☐ | ☐ |
| Do I spend a lot of time controlling others? | ☐ | ☐ | ☐ | ☐ | ☐ |
| I find it hard to stop doing things myself. | ☐ | ☐ | ☐ | ☐ | ☐ |
| I find it difficult to seek feedback on my delegation. | ☐ | ☐ | ☐ | ☐ | ☐ |
| I find it difficult to give negative feedback. | ☐ | ☐ | ☐ | ☐ | ☐ |
| I find it difficult to give positive feedback. | ☐ | ☐ | ☐ | ☐ | ☐ |

For the first three questions if you scored 1 or 2 you may have serious trust and confidence issues that need to be dealt with. For the remaining five questions/statements you may have uncovered some problem areas if you scored 4 or 5.

For inspiration try asking yourself:

- Who is the best delegator I have worked for or have seen? What about their delegation style do I find effective? Can they possibly help me with my own delegation?

d.  What external conditions, if any, are making delegating more difficult for you to do well?

Review this checklist and highlight the barriers that apply to you:

- Too much fire-fighting or urgent work.
- A micromanaging boss.
- Too many new challenges arising.
- Too much incoming information, emails, messages etc.
- Lack of trained staff to delegate to.
- Overstretched staff.

What three changes would make the biggest difference to the value added by your area:

1)_____

2)_____

3)_____

e.  What self-imposed barriers, if any, are affecting the efficiency, effectiveness or economy of your delegation?

Delegation is a classic area in which subconscious beliefs, fears, concerns or overconfidence can adversely affect a manager's actions and delegation style. It is useful to have some understanding of these aspects as they may be keys to knowing you, or someone else you work with, needs help to change effectively.

To simplify, our feelings, fears and memories, both positive and negative, are often held in our subconscious mind. Sometimes we can react to situations based upon these "learned" behaviors and the fact that they are held in our subconscious can mean that we are not overly conscious of their impact. They are often illogical and are part of being human.

Psychological studies of individuals' propensity to make decisions and assume responsibility, as well as their desires to be controlled by others or not, show some common preferences. Among these are:

- People who wish to control as much as possible because they are afraid of failure or things going wrong.

- Those who have a strong desire for recognition and fear if they delegate that someone else will get the credit. They can overstretch themselves in seeking recognition or gratification.

- Some people lack inner confidence and can abdicate control to others as a result.

- Some like to get reassurance from others in relation to making a decision or assuming responsibility.

- They can fear failure or criticism and seek to share responsibility as a result.

- Those that can be loyal but prefer not to assume responsibility, preferring clear instructions and following regulations.

Do you recognize yourself or anyone you have known through your career who may have been affected by any of these psychological aspects? Sometimes we can suspect we are encountering a psychological barrier when we, or others, know that something has to be done differently. We may understand why, but nevertheless find change very difficult or virtually impossible to implement effectively and sustainably.

For any individual there can be challenges of this kind along a career. With experience, feedback and guidance, especially skilled coaching, individuals can help bring these aspects into a healthy balance. We might still feel some vestiges of fear or resistance but we have learned what is right and how to act in a balanced, effective and well-judged way.

Senior people and executives are not always free from some of these issues. Sometimes their drive and energy has in part come from certain inner insecurities. These can drive them on to success up to a certain level but promotions to higher levels can expose their insecurities more clearly and make success harder to achieve at the new, higher and often more strategic level.

It's relatively common to encounter other types of barriers in delegation practices. Let's look into these now.

Note how significant each of the following barriers are for you. A "B" would denote big, an "M" medium, "S" small and "N" not at all.

☐    Lack of trust in others.

☐    Unsure of your role in the organization.

☐    Struggle to let go of tasks you like or are comfortable with.

☐    Fear of the loss of control.

☐    Pride – sustainable success requires team effort.

☐    Prefer routine lonesome tasks to controlling work of others.

☐    Old habits.

☐    Leaving things to the last minute – being too pressure prompted.

☐    Not taking the time to structure and plan work.

☐    Firefighting – giving preference to the urgent over the important and not urgent.

☐    Lost in too many details – not seeing the wood from the trees.

☐    Fear of loss of contact or profile.

☐    Wanting to be visible to or liked by certain people.

☐    Wanting to be involved in everything.

☐     Wanting to appear busy.

☐     The urge to micromanage.

☐     Concern of losing a well-practiced skill.

☐     Uncertainty about other people's roles.

☐     Risk aversion.

What do your self-assessment results tell you? Are there any similarities within your greatest set of barriers? You can use your findings as potential inputs for resolution in section 7.

You should see that you are being realistic. What do your results say about the quality of the outcomes of your delegation? If there are clear issues in relation to these objective outcomes and they have been present for some time, you will be limited in the quality and scope of your delegation. Limitations might be due to circumstances outside of your direct control, but even if this is the case, there are nearly always things you can do to improve the situation.

Write any notes in the space below:

## 6.4    Delegation strengths and development checklist

Here is a useful checklist of items to assess your delegation and that of your team. Circle "S" to indicate this area is one of your strengths. Circle "D" to indicate this area is one of your development needs:

S/D    Achieves desired results and quality outcomes from the team's efforts.

S/D    Follows a sound process but is flexible when appropriate.

S/D    Achieves synergy in a way that the team's output is more valuable than the sum of each individual's potential.

S/D    Skillfully balances the need to get a job or project done with optimal efficiency, economy and effectiveness with balancing the motivational and developmental needs of staff delegated to. Thus increasing staff satisfaction and competence.

S/D    Releases time to make his or her own unique contribution.

S/D    Gains respect as a leader and manager.

S/D    Steps in and out as necessary, with appropriate and clear communication.

S/D    Understands that perfection can be the enemy of good and acts consistently.

S/D    Delegates appropriately, taking into account whether a task is routine, new, highly complex, higher risk or more volatile.

S/D    Understands, supports and challenges different personalities and profiles: i.e., Too independent, too clingy, varying levels of skill and confidence.

S/D    Frees him or herself up for new opportunities as the "bench strength" of the team advance.

S/D    Manages risk appropriately.

S/D    When leading or coordinating projects is able to delegate and control effectively to ensure the critical path is well-established and managed.

S/D    Understands and delegates effectively to ensure the team achieves quick wins when appropriate.

S/D    Understands the Pareto principle - that often 20% of the effort can achieve 80% of the results and leverages this aspect in delegating effectively.

S/D    **Is prepared to delegate important and stretching tasks, adequately judging the needs for developmental challenges and support.**

S/D    Balances trust and control in motivational and practical ways, seeks feedback and input in getting the balance right, but ultimately assumes responsibility for such decisions and judgments.

S/D    **Ensures an appropriate mix and quantity of formal and informal follow-ups.**

S/D    Asks open questions to ascertain confidence and concerns.

S/D    **Reviews completed work projects or assignments for ways to improve effectiveness, efficiency or economy.**

S/D    Learns from errors or undesired outcomes. Seeks ongoing feedback.

S/D    **Can create a sense of urgency as necessary.**

S/D    Manages and delegates well in respect of priorities.

S/D    **Manages and delegates well in respect of what is urgent and important as well as not urgent yet important.**

S/D    Manages well to ensure team time spent on less important matters are minimized through root cause analysis and process management.

# 7. YOUR A TO B ACTION PLAN

### *Step 1*

Review your answers and notes from the guidebook. This will include tips and ideas that you marked as resonating. Consolidate these or highlight the most important aspects in a specific color.

On the Challenge-Priority Brainstorming Chart (see Appendix) list challenges you have picked up from this guidebook, however small they may be.

Stand back from your list and see what links and connections there are – maybe use a different color to highlight challenges that have a similar source such as communication difficulties, fears, feeling incompetent etc.

If possible, group these items under headings or concepts that you think appropriate – use your intuition and creativity here. Go as much with your feelings as your logical mind.

If you have several items for potential action, number them in priority order. There tends to be something we need to address first because it is more important to us or will give us the most benefits.

Take your top priority challenge and move on to your Thrive Action Plan (see Appendix).

### *Step 2*

Take this top grouping/item you identified in your Challenge-Priority Brainstorming Chart. What is the right goal or **B** here? What is going to make the most significant difference?

Try writing the goal down on a separate sheet of paper in three different ways. Which one do you find most compelling? What is it that makes it so? Think about why achieving this goal will help and what you will gain from it.

Studies have shown that people who can create a vivid image of what their achievement will look and feel like are more likely to achieve it.

Take your time to really immerse yourself in this image. What you feel when you think of this image should be used as a tool to motivate yourself along your journey.

### Step 3

Build on the goal to make it SMART:

Specific: As detailed and real as possible – something you can visualize clearly if you are a visual person.

Measurable: Make sure you have quantitative targets for the activity itself and the impact or outcomes you want too.

Attainable: You sense it's a stretch but you know you can do it!

Realistic: Think of the practical aspects that are necessary for success – the resources, support, strategies and tactics that will bring you success. You should be able to list these on the Thrive Action Plan, if you struggle then your goal is possibly not realistic enough.

Timed: Build in specific deadlines – for the big steps and completion. These can be further broken down into daily or weekly goals if, for example, you need to grow your comfort zone bit by bit, day by day. Think stepping stones!

Example of a SMART delegation improvement goal:

"I will be recognized by my direct reports as a good delegator, and consequently, a much improved developer of people within four months. This will see me working 40 hours a week on average, 15 hours a week less than currently and 2.5 hours more than the average of my reports. I will increasingly play towards my strength in developing and managing people towards the business strategy. I shall commence with a team meeting next week on a work reallocation that better plays to the individual talents and experience of the team and that has agreed criteria on fairness."

### Step 4

Get going on your first action. This should be within a week from now.

*Step 5*

You need to get the support resources lined up.

It helps if you can inform a few well selected individuals from your colleagues, friends or family to share the goal with, seek their feedback and suggestions of how you can do things better and achieve your goal. As you move forward they can give you further valuable feedback on your progress as well as encouragement.

Think about who encourages you best, who gives you the best advice, who helps you when you are in difficulty and who may have the same developmental challenge and can go on the journey with you. Avoid sharing your goal with negative or cynical people who are likely only to discourage you.

Decide on who are the best people to help you: usually a group of 1-3 mentors.

*Step 6*

As we investigated in section 6.3 of this guidebook there will be self-imposed barriers to your success in delegating to others. What were the main ones you highlighted? Think also about how you plan to overcome these inevitable barriers and how you can use your support system to push you past these!

*Step 7*

Decide on the frequency you are going to review your progress towards your goal – often weekly works well. What has worked well and what lessons have been learned?

Build on the successes and lessons learned and plan your next week's activity.

If you get discouraged or have a setback, don't be too hard on yourself. This can happen. After doing something that leaves you feeling positive and relaxed, build on the positive momentum to press forward with your goals. Look for inspiration in this guidebook.

Be determined to take some positives out of the setback.

Ask if your goal or your sub-steps are too stretched and you need to re-calibrate or take longer. Sometimes behavioral change programs can take nine months or so!

If you really get stuck, seek help from a good mentor or coach.

Keep going.

*Step 8*

Success! Well done.

# 8. KEY POINT SUMMARY

With this guidebook you hopefully have realized there is much more to delegation than giving orders. Good delegation can be a source of competitive advantage, motivation, time-saving, efficient operations and employee skill development. Who would have thought so much can be achieved by simply improving the manner in which we give tasks to those around us? The extensive self-assessments on your personal barriers will hopefully have given you a few clues as to what things need to be tackled in your action plan. Hopefully the tips provided within this guidebook will help you build trust and make your team and company more efficient. Good luck!

# 9. USEFUL EXTRA READING

Motivating people well is essential in delegating effectively over long periods of time. Employees may differ in their intrinsic motivations or become tired of your style of managing people. The *A to B Guide to Motivation* tackles these issues and more.

If you or your employees struggle with procrastination and forming a cohesive plan to perform delegated tasks, you will enjoy reading the *A to B Guide to Prioritization*.

Did the sections on delegating upwards or the importance of delegation in succession management resonate with you? The *A to B Guide to Dealing with Difficult Bosses* and *A to B Guide to Office Politics* will give you further guidance in these areas.

### References and recommendations:

Amar, A. D., Carsten Hentrich and Vlatka Hlupic. "To Be a Better Leader, Give Up Authority" Harvard Business Review. 01 Dec. 2009. Web. 01 Mar. 2012. <http://www.hbr.org/2009/12/to-be-a-better-leader-give-up-authority/ar/1>

Covey, Stephen R. *Seven Habits of Highly Effective People*. New York: Free Press, 2 Nov. 2004. Print.

Handy, Charles B. *Understanding Organizations*. London: Penguin Books Ltd, 25 Feb. 1993. Print.

Ryan, Leo Robert. *Clinical Interpretation of the FIRO-B*. Palo Alto: Consulting Psychologists Press, 1989. Print.

# ABOUT THE AUTHOR

Brian Guest is a former CEO with an extensive international career in Fortune 100 companies. Based on his experience working at various management levels and motivated by a desire to help others achieve their potential he decided to begin a career as an international executive coach.

He obtained an M.A. in Natural Sciences from the University of Cambridge, England, in 1978. Brian is also qualified as an ACA (Chartered Accountant, the UK equivalent of a CPA) in 1981.

In 1982 he began his international career on joining the American International Group (then a Fortune 100 company, the largest global insurer) as an international auditor. He was promoted to audit management and worked in the USA, Latin America, Caribbean, Europe and Africa.

In 1987 he joined Royal Insurance (now RSA) and worked in financial management in the international division.

Joining Commercial Union (now Aviva plc, 2011 Fortune Global 500 number 64) three years later, he worked in business development, holding various positions including being the General Manager for Hong Kong and Regional Director for Latin America.

In 1997 he began working in the HSBC Group (2011 Fortune Global 500 number 46) and his responsibilities over an eight year period included being CEO for the US$500mn Brazilian insurance business with 1,500 staff as well as Chief Underwriting Officer for Latin America. During this time his division received two national prizes for best performing insurer.

# APPENDIX

# CHALLENGE-PRIORITY BRAINSTORMING CHART

What are my challenges/problem areas?

Why are they challenges? What specific problems need to be addressed?

Can I divide my challenges/problem areas into categories?

| Challenge | Priority |
| --- | --- |
|  |  |

# THRIVE ACTION PLAN

| 1. Challenge | What challenge am I addressing? |
|---|---|
| 2. Goals | Based on my challenge, what goal can I set myself?<br><br><br>Do I have a motivating image of the final result? Yes/No |
| 3. SMART Goals | Use the SMART goals system to build on your goal. Specific details:<br><br><br><br>How will I measure it?<br><br><br>Time frames & deadlines:<br><br>Is my goal attainable and realistic? Yes/No |
| 4. First Step | My first step towards achieving this goal is...<br><br>By when? |
| 5. Support System | Who will be my mentors/support? What skills and resources do I have? Do I need any additional training? |
| 6. Barriers | Possible barriers that could get in my way: |
| 7. Review | Frequency of progress reviews & contingency plan: |

# ADDITIONAL NOTES

www.ingramcontent.com/pod-product-compliance
Lightning Source LLC
Chambersburg PA
CBHW060645210326
41520CB00010B/1745